# Caring for Your
# Rabbit

Jill Foran

**Weigl Publishers Inc.**

**Project Coordinator**
Diana Marshall

**Design and Layout**
Warren Clark
Katherine Phillips

**Copy Editor**
Jennifer Nault

**Photo Research**
Gayle Murdoff

Locate the rabbit paw prints throughout the book to find useful tips on caring for your pet.

Published by Weigl Publishers Inc.
123 South Broad Street, Box 227
Mankato, MN 56002 USA
Web site: www.weigl.com

### Library of Congress Cataloging-in-Publication Data

Foran, Jill.
  Caring for your rabbit / Jill Foran.
      v. cm. -- (Caring for your pet)
Contents: Bunny basics -- Pet profiles -- From food to friend -- Rabbit life cycles -- Picking your rabbit -- Supplies and equipment -- Rabbit food -- Getting to know your rabbit -- Bunny brushing -- Keeping your rabbit healthy -- Bunny behavior -- Legendary rabbits.
  ISBN 1-59036-034-6 (lib. bdg. : alk. paper)
 1.  Rabbits--Juvenile literature. [1. Rabbits as pets. 2. Pets.]  I. Title. II. Caring for your pet (Mankato, Minn.)
  SF453.2 .F67 2002
  636.9'322--dc21

                          2002006157

Printed in the United States
3 4 5 6 7 8 9 0   06 05 04

**Photograph and Text Credits**
Every reasonable effort has been made to trace ownership and to obtain permission to reprint copyright material. The publishers would be pleased to have any errors or omissions brought to their attention so that they may be corrected in subsequent printings.

**Cover:** lop rabbit (Reneé Stockdale); **Behling and Johnson Photography:** title page, pages 3, 5, 6 right, 7 left, 8, 11 top, 11 bottom, 13; **Comstock Images:** pages 23, 31; **Corel Corporation:** page 29; **Lorraine Hill:** pages 7 middle, 7 right, 10 top; **Eric Ilasenko Photo/Digital:** pages 6 left, 6 middle; **Picturesof.net:** page 28; **Reneé Stockdale:** pages 4, 9, 10 bottom, 12, 14, 15, 16, 17, 18/19, 20, 21 top, 21 bottom, 22, 24, 25, 27, 30; ©**Warner Bros/Photofest:** page 26.

White, Rosalyn. *The Rabbit in the Moon*. Berkeley: Dharma Publishing, 1989.

# Contents

# Bunny Basics

Humans have kept rabbits as pets for hundreds of years. Rabbits are lovable, social animals. Rabbits make great pets because they are clean, smart, and quiet. They do not need constant attention, but enjoy plenty of cuddling time with their owners. They can also be very entertaining to watch. From thumping their hind legs to rolling over on their back, rabbits have many ways of communicating with the humans they love.

Rabbits are very delicate animals. They need to be treated gently.

■■■ For many people, rabbits are perfect furry companions.

## Fascinating Facts

- More than 12 million rabbits are raised in the United States every year.
- A male rabbit is called a buck. A female rabbit is called a doe.

While rabbits may be cute and quiet, they are also a big responsibility. Once you choose a rabbit, you must care for your pet for the rest of her life. This means you must provide her with the things she needs to be happy and healthy. Rabbits require a large shelter, called a hutch, in which to live. Rabbits also need a balanced diet, regular **grooming**, and plenty of exercise. Visits to the **veterinarian** are needed to keep your rabbit healthy. If you give your rabbit the love she needs and deserves, she will return your love in many ways.

■■■ Rabbits must be kept away from stressful situations because they are timid and easily frightened.

# Pet Profiles

Rabbits come in a variety of colors, shapes, sizes, and coats. There are more than fifty **breeds** of **domestic** rabbits around the world. There are even more mixed breeds. Mixed-breed rabbits come from parents that are of different breeds. Purebred rabbits come from known relatives. In purebred rabbits, traits, such as ear shape or fur type, can be traced through the generations.

## NETHERLAND DWARF

- Smallest breed of rabbit
- Weighs 2 to 3 pounds when full-grown
- Comes in a wide range of colors
- Cute, round body
- Large eyes and short ears
- Popular pets, but not good with very small children

## DUTCH

- One of the most popular pet rabbit breeds
- Friendly, mild nature
- Comes in a variety of colors, but is known for its special white markings
- Females are gentle and attentive mothers
- Weighs about 4 to 5 pounds when full-grown

## MINI REX

- Thick, velvety coat
- Nicknamed "the velveteen rabbit"
- About fifteen different colors, including white
- Very friendly
- Also comes in a larger size, called standard Rex

Whether they are mixed breed or purebred, all pet rabbits have special features that make them attractive to their owners. Some rabbits are friendlier than others. Some types of rabbits will require a great deal of grooming, while others will not. Knowing the features of each type of rabbit will help you to choose your perfect pet.

## ENGLISH ANGORA

- On average, English Angoras weigh 7 pounds when full-grown
- Long, white coat, which consists of wool instead of fur
- Wool can grow as long as 10 inches
- Quiet and slow moving
- Requires a great deal of grooming

## LOP

- Long, limp, hanging "lop" ears and thick body
- Large, round head and flat face
- Long, dense coat
- Comes in a variety of solid and broken colors
- Quiet and mild in manner
- Neck is hidden

## CALIFORNIAN

- Compact body
- Friendly, gentle personality
- Red eyes
- Ears, feet, tail, and nose can be blue, black, brown, or lilac in color
- Rest of the body is white
- Alert and active

# Bunny Background

**R**abbits have been around for a long time. Scientists have found ancient **fossils** that suggest that rabbits have lived on Earth for more than 40 million years. During this time, the main features of the rabbit have changed very little. Many **species** of rabbits have lived during this period. One of these species is called the European wild rabbit. This species still lives wild in Europe and Africa.

When young children are playing with a rabbit, they should always be supervised by an adult.

■ Almost all of the domestic rabbit breeds in the world are related to the European wild rabbit.

## Fascinating Facts

- Cave paintings of rabbits dating back to the **Stone Age** have been found in Spain.
- Rabbits are crepuscular. This means that they are most active at dawn and dusk.
- All rabbits belong to a group called lagomorphs, which means "hare-like" in the Greek language.

Early peoples hunted European wild rabbits for food and sport. As time passed, people began to realize the usefulness of raising rabbits for their meat, skin, and fur. Early European explorers brought rabbits on their voyages because these animals were a good food source. By the 1800s, people in many parts of the world had realized that these rabbits also made friendly pets. Owners who had once farmed rabbits for food began developing new breeds.

■ Explorers introduced the European wild rabbit to many of the new places they discovered, including parts of North America.

# Life Cycle

Rabbits have a life span of about 8 to 10 years. With great care, many rabbits can live much longer. Throughout his lifetime, your pet rabbit will depend on you to give him proper care and love. From newborn to full-grown, your pet rabbit will have specific needs at different stages of his life.

## Newborn Rabbits

Rabbits are tiny and helpless when they are born. They have no fur and their eyes remain closed for several days. Newborn rabbits cuddle together in their nest for warmth. They are not yet ready to be handled by humans.

## Six Months

By 6 months, most rabbits are full-grown. They are also old enough to mate. Rabbits at this age and older are very active and social. They require plenty of exercise and attention.

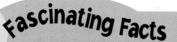

## Fascinating Facts

- Newborn rabbits are called kittens.
- There are usually six to eight kittens in one litter of rabbits.

## Two to Five Weeks

By this age, baby rabbits will begin to come out of the nest and explore. Their fur will have grown, and their eyes will have opened. They continue to drink their mother's milk. Around this time, they begin to play together and to nibble on solid food. The best time for humans to start handling baby rabbits is when the rabbits are 3 weeks of age.

## Eight to Ten Weeks

By 8 weeks, young rabbits are ready to be weaned. This means they are ready to stop drinking their mother's milk. They will start eating only solid food. Around this time, rabbits are also ready to be separated from their mother and littermates. If they are not separated, they may begin to fight. Never buy a rabbit that is too young. Rabbits should not be separated from their mothers until they are about 8 weeks old.

# Picking Your Pet

**B**efore selecting your rabbit, there are many important factors to consider. Your answers to the following questions will help you to determine the pet rabbit that is best for you.

## Where Should I Get My Rabbit?

You can get a rabbit from a breeder, an animal shelter, or a pet store. Perhaps the best place to buy a rabbit is from a private breeder. Most breeders work hard to raise healthy rabbits. If you buy your rabbit from a breeder, you will know exactly how old the rabbit is. Animal shelters find homes for abandoned animals. They ensure that the animals will make suitable pets. If you choose to buy your rabbit from a pet store, find a reliable store with a well-informed staff.

Before bringing a new rabbit home, make sure that none of your family members have pet allergies.

■ Shelters provide information on how to care for each rabbit.

Mixed Breed

Name: Buns

Sex: Female/Spayed  Age: 6 years

Reason for surrender: Not enough time

Notes: Buns is an older rabbit who needs a quiet loving home. She enjoys being petted and scratched. She is just a little timid and would love a gentle loving person who understands she's not as young as she used to be.

Health: Buns had extremely long nails and a torn toe nail. She has healed well. It is important to keep her nails trimmed back. She was

# Which Rabbit Breed Should I Buy?

It is important to choose the breed that is best for you. Research a number of the rabbit breeds you like. By doing this, you can learn about any special requirements the breeds may have. Angora breeds need extra grooming. **Albino** rabbits cannot tolerate bright light. If there are young children in your family, a medium- to large-sized breed is best. Dwarf rabbits and other small breeds are difficult to handle. They tend to struggle and panic when they are picked up.

# What Do I Have Time For?

A pet rabbit takes a great deal of commitment. All rabbits need love, attention, and exercise. They need to be watched when they are out of their hutches. Rabbits need to be groomed. They must also have their hutches regularly cleaned.

■■■ Be sure that you will have plenty of time to spend with a pet before you buy your rabbit.

## Fascinating Facts

- Rabbits born in the summer months develop larger ears than rabbits born in cooler months. This allows them to cool themselves more easily.
- There are more breeds of rabbits than of any other domestic animal, except the dog.

# Happy in a Hutch

**M**oving to a new home can be stressful for any creature, including a rabbit. To help ease your new bunny's nervousness, it is a good idea to be prepared with some basic supplies. One of the most important items for your rabbit is a hutch. Many people believe that wire hutches are the best type of shelter because they are the easiest to clean. Wood hutches are also very popular. If you want to keep your rabbit outside, a wood hutch provides better protection from the weather. The hutch should give him plenty of space to move around in. It should have a daytime play area and a separate sleeping compartment.

Never put anything made of plastic in the hutch. Your rabbit may chew it and swallow pieces that she cannot digest.

You can either buy a hutch at a pet supply store or build one yourself.

Your rabbit's hutch is his home, so try to make the space as comfortable as possible. If the hutch has a solid floor, it should be covered with clean wood shavings, which are **absorbent**. Wood shavings, along with hay, can be used for bedding material. Your rabbit's home should also be equipped with a large water bottle, wood for **gnawing**, and a food bowl that is heavy enough that it will not tip. Brushes for grooming and toys to keep your rabbit fit are also essential supplies.

■■■ For a 6-pound rabbit, a hutch should be at least 48 inches long, 30 inches wide, and 18 inches high.

## Fascinating Facts

- Rabbits can be trained to use a litter box. Since rabbits tend to go to the bathroom in one corner of the hutch, a litter box should be placed in your pet's corner of choice for easy training.
- Rabbits can run as fast as 35 miles per hour in short bursts. They can jump as high as 3 feet.

# Rabbit Food

Rabbits are herbivores. This means that their diet is entirely plant matter. They do not eat meat. Store-bought rabbit pellets are the easiest way to provide proper nutrition for your rabbit. These special pellets are available at most pet supply stores and many supermarkets. Your rabbit's diet should also be **supplemented** with fresh fruit and vegetables, as well as plenty of hay, which helps digestion.

Always give new foods to your rabbit in small amounts. Too much of a new food will likely cause your rabbit to be sick.

■ Although they only eat plants, rabbits still require a balanced diet in order to stay healthy.

The amount of food your pet rabbit requires depends on her size, age, and breed, but all rabbits should be fed once or twice a day. Be sure to always fill your pet rabbit's bowl at the same time every day. Rabbits are creatures of habit. They are happiest when a routine has been set. Also, provide your rabbit with a constant supply of fresh water. A rabbit should never be without fresh water.

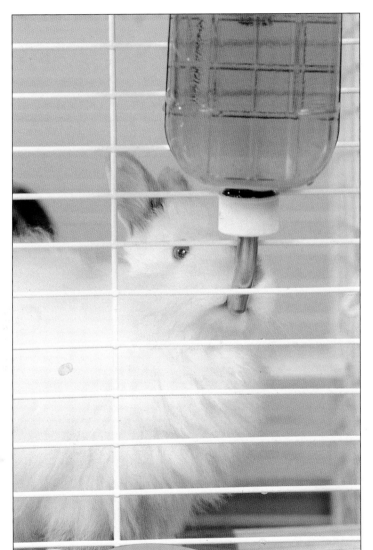

Without water, rabbits do not digest their food properly.

## Fascinating Facts

- Chocolate is poisonous to rabbits. Other foods that are harmful to rabbits include iceberg lettuce, cabbage, broccoli, and anything sugary.
- Rabbits have a better sense of taste than humans. A rabbit's tongue has 17,000 taste buds, while a human's tongue has 10,000.

# Furry and Floppy

There are more than twenty-five species of rabbits in the world. Some of the most common species found in North America include the cottontail, the jackrabbit, and the domestic rabbit. While rabbits come in many sizes, shapes, and colors, they all share a number of physical characteristics. They all have long ears, short tails, and delicate skeletons. In the wild, their features help rabbits move quickly and quietly to avoid being eaten by **predators**.

A rabbit has scent glands near his bottom, and beneath his chin. When a rabbit wants to mark his territory, he uses these glands to release a distinctive scent.

Rabbits have long hind legs and shorter front legs. When a rabbit runs, his hind legs touch the ground before his front legs. Unlike cats or dogs, rabbits do not have protective pads on the bottoms of their paws. Rabbits only have fur for protection.

A rabbit relies greatly on her ears. Not only do the ears allow a rabbit to hear sounds from all directions, they also keep her body temperature constant. Rabbits do not have sweat glands. Instead, their ears contain blood vessels that cool the rabbit when she is too hot.

Rabbits have keen eyesight. They can detect movement from a long distance. They also have a third eyelid that protects their eyes from hazards, such as dust storms or fights with other animals. The eyes are located on the sides the head, allowing rabbits to see to the side, above, and behind.

A rabbit has an excellent sense of smell. Her nose has millions of scent **receptors** that detect all kinds of odors. A rabbit will twitch her nose 20 to 120 times a minute. This allows her to expose more scent receptors and detect more smells.

The whiskers on a rabbit's face are very long. A rabbit uses his whiskers to touch things that are close to his face, and to feel his way around in the dark.

 **LOP**

A rabbit's mouth holds twenty-eight teeth. Of these, twenty-two teeth are **molars,** and six are **incisors**. A rabbit's teeth continue to grow throughout the animal's life. Chewing and gnawing usually wears the teeth down and keeps them at a proper length.

# Bunny Brushing

Rabbits enjoy being clean, and most will groom themselves several times a day. This continuous grooming keeps rabbits looking and feeling their best, but it can also be harmful. Rabbits can get hairballs if they swallow too much fur when they are licking themselves. This is dangerous because, unlike cats, rabbits cannot vomit. As a result, large hairballs can block a rabbit's stomach, making him unable to eat and digest food. To prevent this from happening, brush your rabbit on a regular basis. Long-haired rabbits will require more grooming than short-haired rabbits.

Do not bathe your rabbit unless your veterinarian tells you to do so. Baths lower rabbits' body temperatures to dangerous levels.

The more fur you remove through brushing, the less fur your pet rabbit will swallow.

It is very important to be as gentle as possible when grooming your pet. Rabbits have very delicate skin, and rough brushing or combing can tear or scratch it. Use a soft brush and plastic comb. Always brush in the same direction that the fur grows. The time that you spend grooming your rabbit is valuable. Not only is it fun, it also gives you the opportunity to check that your pet's skin and fur is clean and healthy.

■ Like cats, rabbits use their tongues and paws to clean their bodies.

## Fascinating Facts

- A rabbit's incisors grow at a rate of about 5 inches per year. If his teeth do not wear down properly, a veterinarian can file them down. Rabbits' claws also grow quickly and must to be trimmed on a regular basis. Never try trimming your pet's claws without first having your veterinarian show you how it is done.
- Rabbits shed their coats about every 3 months. While some rabbits shed their fur within a few days, others can take weeks to lose their old coats.
- The only breed of rabbit that does not groom itself is the Angora rabbit.

# Healthy and Happy

**R**abbits are generally healthy animals. If they are properly cared for, they will very rarely become sick. In order to keep your rabbit healthy, be sure to feed her a balanced diet. Pet rabbits require regular grooming. It is also important to clean your rabbit's hutch two to three times a week. By cleaning your pet's home regularly, you are removing germs that could make your rabbit sick. Some rabbits may fall ill if they experience stressful situations. Owners can help prevent these situations from happening. They can make sure that their pet's hutch is protected from other animals. They can also keep the hutch away from loud noises, direct sunlight, and damp conditions.

Rabbits love to chew. Make sure that all electrical cords and poisonous plants are far from your rabbit's reach.

■ Rabbits are very active animals. They need plenty of exercise time outside their hutch.

Sometimes rabbits become sick even when they are well cared for. By observing your rabbit closely when it is healthy, you will probably notice when something seems wrong. Signs of a sick rabbit include loss of appetite, inactivity, and dull eyes and fur. If you notice any of these symptoms, or any other changes in your rabbit's behavior, bring your pet to a veterinarian right away.

■ To keep your pet rabbit healthy, take him to the veterinarian for a checkup at least once a year.

## Fascinating Facts

- The most common illness in rabbits is called snuffles. Rabbit snuffles is similar to the common cold that humans catch.
- The normal body temperature of a rabbit is between 101.5° and 104° Fahrenheit.
- Pet rabbits may be **vaccinated** to prevent them from catching the common rabbit diseases. Ask your veterinarian about vaccinations.

# Bunny Behavior

Rabbits are very social animals. In the wild, they live in large groups called warrens. Their social nature makes domestic rabbits great pets. They get along well with humans and other animals. However, rabbits are easily frightened. They must be introduced to new people and other pets slowly. In order to tame your rabbit, it is important to begin by handling her frequently for short periods of time. Too much handling will make your rabbit nervous, which can cause her to become sick.

Never pick your rabbit up by her ears. It is very painful for the rabbit, and can cause damage to the muscles and membranes in the ear.

Rabbits should never be left alone for long periods of time. Their intense curiosity can get them into trouble.

## Pet Peeves

**Rabbits do not like:**
- taking a bath
- being too hot or too cold
- loud noises
- changes to their routine
- having their feet tickled
- not enough playtime
- having their ears pulled
- not having enough privacy
- being chased

Try not to startle your rabbit. When taking your rabbit out of her hutch, slowly approach her from the front and speak to her with a soft, soothing voice. When your rabbit appears calm and ready to be handled, gently pick her up. The best way to pick up a rabbit is to hold her by the skin at the back of the neck with one hand, and to slide the other hand under her body to support her weight. Hold the rabbit close to your body so that she feels safe and secure.

Most rabbits love to play and will often try to include their owners in their games. Rabbits also love to learn and can easily be trained to do many things. They enjoy sitting on a warm lap and cuddling as well.

■ Once your rabbit is comfortable in her new home, you will start to get to know her personality.

## Fascinating Facts

- Rabbits are ground-dwellers. This means that they are very scared of heights.
- A rabbit can easily break her back if she kicks hard while her rear legs are being held. Rabbits should always be handled very gently.
- Rabbits thump their hind legs to get attention or to warn others of possible danger.

# Leaping Legends

Throughout history, humans have felt a special fondness for rabbits. Aside from seeing these animals as a source of food and fur, people around the world have also admired rabbits for their intelligence and beauty. Many cultures have legends and customs that honor the rabbit. Iroquois Peoples pay tribute to the rabbit with a special dance. Several Eastern European cultures believe that the figure of a rabbit can be seen in the moon. This figure is said to rule over all of the rabbits on Earth.

■ Bugs Bunny greeted every new experience with the phrase, "Eh, what's up, Doc?"

## Fascinating Facts

- One of the world's favorite legendary rabbits is Bugs Bunny. This fun-loving rabbit has been featured in children's cartoons since the 1940s.
- Rabbits have long been popular book subjects. Classic children's books such as *The Tale of Peter Rabbit* and *The Velveteen Rabbit* are read around the world.

One of the world's most legendary rabbits is the Easter bunny. Every year on Easter Sunday, children all over North America and Europe search eagerly for eggs left behind by this holiday rabbit. The Easter bunny appears in an ancient German legend. According to this legend, Eastre, the Goddess of Spring, turns a bird into a rabbit every year once spring has arrived. Since ancient times, humans have linked rabbits with spring, **fertility**, and new life.

■ In some legends, rabbits were given the gift of laying eggs once a year.

## Rabbit in the Moon

The "Rabbit in the Moon" is an East Indian fable about generosity. One day, the Lord of Heaven arrives disguised as an old wanderer. He is tired and hungry. He asks three friends if they can find him something to eat. The monkey brings nuts, and the fox brings fish, but the rabbit cannot find anything. The rabbit is very sad that he has failed to find anything for the visitor's meal. He asks the monkey to gather some wood. Then, he asks the fox to light a fire with the wood. Suddenly, the rabbit says "Please eat me" and throws himself into the flames. The Lord of Heaven is so impressed by the rabbit's selfless action that he takes the rabbit's body to heaven to be buried in the Palace of the Moon. Some people believe that they can still see a rabbit on the moon.

From Rosalyn White's *The Rabbit in the Moon*.

# Pet Puzzlers

What do you know about rabbits?
If you can answer the following
questions correctly, you may
be ready to own a pet rabbit.

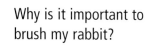

**Q** Why is it important to brush my rabbit?

Rabbits, like cats, can swallow too much fur while grooming themselves. Hairballs can block their stomach, preventing them from eating. Regular brushing can decrease hairballs and keep rabbits' fur healthy.

**Q** How long do pet rabbits live?

Rabbits generally live to be 8 to 10 years of age. Healthy, happy pet rabbits have been known to live much longer.

**Q** When did the relationship between rabbits and humans begin?

Cave paintings that date back to the Stone Age have been found in Spain. These paintings are the earliest recorded signs of the relationship between rabbits and humans.

**Q** What is a hutch?

All pet rabbits must have a hutch to live in. A hutch is a large cage designed for an animal like a rabbit. This can be bought at a pet supply store or built.

**Q** Do rabbits eat meat?

Rabbits are herbivores, which means that they eat only plants. Rabbits should never be fed meat.

**Q** How often should a pet rabbit be fed?

Veterinarians recommend that pet rabbits be fed once or twice a day. The amount of food will vary according to your rabbit's size and breed. Rabbits should be fed at the same time every day.

## Ready for a Rabbit

Before you buy your pet rabbit, write down some rabbit names that you like. Some names may work better for a female rabbit. Others may suit a male rabbit. Here are just a few suggestions:

Charlie

Flopsy

Daisy

Rosie

Thumper

Snowy

Bugs

Fudge

Peter

Molly

# Frequently Asked Questions

### Should I have my rabbit spayed or neutered?

Spaying females and neutering males are operations that make it impossible for rabbits to produce babies. If you do not want your bunny to mate and have babies, it is a good idea to have your pet spayed or neutered. Every year, millions of unwanted rabbits end up in animal shelters because owners could not find homes for their pet's babies. Spayed and neutered rabbits are generally healthier and friendlier than those that can produce babies.

### Should I keep my rabbit inside or outside?

There are many good reasons for keeping your rabbit in your home rather than outside. Rabbits that live inside tend to live longer than outdoor rabbits. This is because they are not exposed to extreme weather or stressful situations. If you keep your rabbit outside, be sure that his hutch is protected from other animals and bad weather.

### Why does my bunny click her teeth?

Rabbits have many ways of communicating their feelings. Tooth clicking usually occurs when a rabbit is being petted or when she is very comfortable. Tooth clicking sounds much like a cat's purring. It means that your rabbit is content.

# More Information

## Animal Organizations

You can help rabbits stay healthy and happy by learning more about them. Many organizations are dedicated to teaching people how to care for and protect their pet pals. For more rabbit information, write to the following organizations:

American Rabbit Breeders Association
P.O. Box 426
Bloomington, IL  61702

Humane Society of the United States
2100 L Street N.W.
Washington, DC  20037

## Web Sites

To answer more of your rabbit questions, go online and surf to the following Web sites:

**Care for Animals**
www.avma.org/careforanimals/
animatedjourneys/animatedfl.asp

**House Rabbit Society**
www.rabbit.org/kids/index.html

**Pet Place**
www.petplace.com

# Words to Know

**absorbent:** able to soak up substances and smells

**albino:** an animal with colorless, or white, fur and pink eyes

**breeds:** groups of animals that share specific characteristics

**domestic:** tamed and used to living among people; not living in the wild

**fertility:** ability to produce babies

**fossils:** remains of animals and plants from long ago found in rocks

**gnawing:** wearing away by nonstop biting or chewing

**grooming:** cleaning by removing dirt and tangles from fur

**incisors:** front teeth used for cutting, tearing, or chewing

**molars:** broad teeth used for grinding

**predators:** animals that hunt and kill other animals for food

**receptors:** sensitive nerve endings

**species:** a group of individuals that shares biological features

**Stone Age:** a period of early human history that lasted from about 2.5 million years ago to about 2400 BC

**supplemented:** added to make complete or whole; improved

**vaccinated:** injected with medicines that help prevent certain diseases

**veterinarian:** animal doctor

# Index